For Tl
Love Of Animals

Volume One

First published in Great Britain by Amazon 2025.
Copyright rests with each individual author and artist.
The moral rights of the authors and artists have been asserted.

ISBN: 9798268684421

Collated and edited by Dawn Wilkinson

Printed in the UK

Illustrations not attributed to an artist in this book were created using Canva and Canva AI

Back page artwork provided by Laura Young

All profits from the sale of this anthology will help provide pet-food bank set ups in the community.
Donations will also be made to local animal charities.

Please join our Facebook group;
For The Love Of Animals,
for more details.

"*Taking any animal into your life will inevitably end in heart-ache, but you don't worry about the hangover when you're at the party.*"

Paul O'Grady

CONTENTS

Foreword By Dawn Wilkinson   9
The Perfect Team By Graham Bell   10
Zebra Artwork By Julie Scott   12
Dog Artwork By Kathleen Casson   14
Poisoned Food By Jo Woodfield   15
Our Dog Trevor By Elaine Gardner   16
Tiger Artwork By John Brookes   18
My Cat Ben By Linda Simcox   20
Elvis Artwork By Jane Kemp   22
Tortoise Artwork By Norma Patterson   24
You Saved Me By Wendy Jackson   25
Butterfly By Julie Meredith   26
Peggy Mace By Becks Macey   28
Rhino Artwork By Philip Barclay   30
Encounter By George Richardson   31
Soulmate By Mo Mitchell   32
Portrait of Maisie By Paul Mitchell   33
Wolf Artwork By Laura Young   34
Hungry Like The Wolf By Dawn Wilkinson   35
The Platypus - A Reet Canny Beast By
Aidan K Morrisey   36
The Kitten And His Paws By Sue Gray   38
Shandy By Margaret Rose   39
Words Are Not Needed By Jackie
Waddington   40
Fancy That By Mary Naylor   41

Little Jenny Wren By Joyce Conway 42

The Peacock By Sheila Berry 45

Photographs By Steve Murray 46

Stag Artwork By Anne Cato 48

Squirrel Artwork By Tess Roxborough 49

Squirrel Poem By John Oxton 49

I'd Rather Have A Dog By Donna Peat 50

Cat Memories By Linda Merritt 52

Sign By Martin Wardle 54

Portrait of Pippa By Rebecca Wardle 55

China By Steve Gore 56

Roxy By Maureen Waters 57

Charlie and Milo By Karen Marchetto 58

Horse Artwork By Ben Tasker 60

Cat Artwork By Ged Hazlehurst 61

Be More Dog By Liam Overend 62

Safari Photographs By Christiane Shillito 64

There Was A Young Boy By Steve Wraith 66

The Guardian By Simon Waim 67

Maple By Grace Hedley 70

Dido By Pip Underwood 71

Bruno By Alice Hedley 72

Bob By Leanne Rooney 73

A Moment's Trance By James Bridgewood 74

Milo By Jo Crawford 76

Pandemonium By Clare McAndrew 77

Artwork By Chris Younger 79

Maisie By Lesley Armour 80

Eric By Helen Aitchison 82

Ode To Cranes By Andy Allum   84
Cheekie By Barry Martin   85
Riverbank By Angela Craddock   86
ORNITHORHYNCUS ANATINUS By Kenn
Creen   88
Best Friends Artwork By Phyllis Benoist   90
Jasper Foreword By Dawn Wilkinson   91
Jasper By Clare Metcalf   92
Thankyou   97

"Until one has loved an animal, a part of one's soul remains unawakened"

Anatole France

Foreword

I would like to express my heartfelt gratitude to everyone who has contributed poetry, short stories, and artwork for this book. As an animal lover, this initiative was inspired by the desire to support local animal charities and establish pet food banks. These efforts aim to help individuals facing short-term financial challenges by alleviating some of their burdens. Animals play a crucial role in enhancing our mental well-being, and it is essential that we do everything possible to ensure people continue to experience the joy and companionship that pets provide. Thank you for joining me in this endeavour to make a positive impact on both people and animals in our communities.

Dawn Wilkinson

The Perfect Team

They walk together on the hill
morning skies are bright and clear,
his stride is purposeful and long,
she's always one step to the rear,
he scans the purple heather vista,
his eyes are focused on his task,
she watches every move he makes
alert to do his bidding should he ask,
she loves this man with all her heart,
she gives her love without condition,
craves the smallest crumb of kindness given
is crushed by slightest hint of admonition.

The sheep are strewn across the hill
and needing moved to pastures green,
"way bye noo Jess " he rasps,
like a bullet from a gun she moves
over bracken, moss and rock and stream,
"gan oot wide!", she arcs away,
glides across the dusty heather,
they cock their lugs her woolly prey,
as instinct drives them all to flock together,
"steady noo ", she checks her speed,
with stealth and guile she brings them forward,
one lifts it's head to break away,
she anticipates and keeps them coming homeward.

The day is done, the race is run,
by his fireside he sits contented,
she lies there stretched out at his feet,
rich reward for service rendered,
but in her mind she's out there still,
her paws they twitch in animation,
in her dreams she runs across the hill
and the vast expanse of her imagination.

Graham Bell

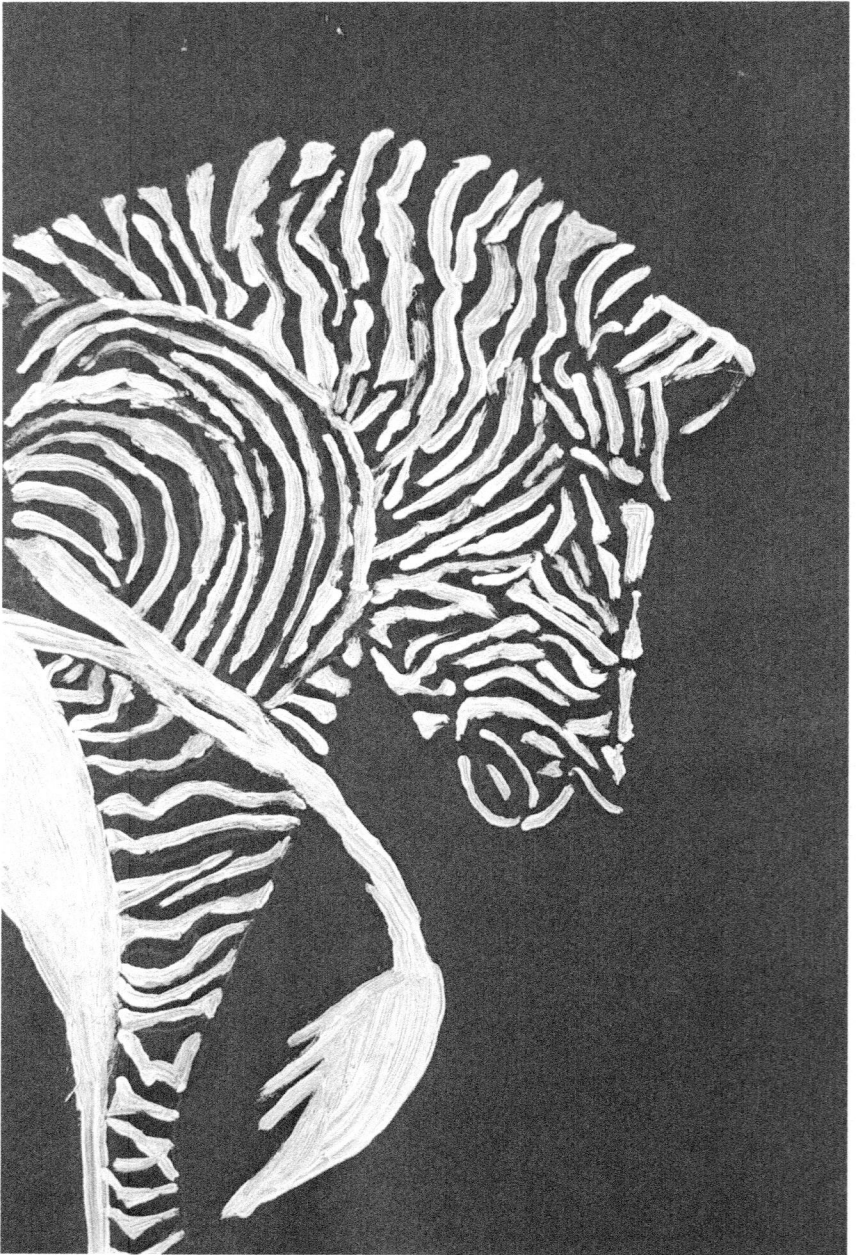

Julie Scott

"I asked the Zebra, 'Are you black with white stripes? Or white with black stripes?' And the zebra asked me, 'Are you good with bad habits? Or are you bad with good habits?"

Shel Silverstein

The zebra does not hide in a herd; it stands out, showing the power of individuality and authenticity

"If a dog will not come to you after having looked you in the face, you should go home and examine your conscience."

Woodrow Wilson

Kathleen Casson

Poisoned Food

I like to see you serve my food
Because that way I know it's good
I love how you feed me
And never deceive me
You know I'm not greedy
Just very needy

Poem and Drawing
By J Woodfield

Our dog Trevor

Our son Connor wanted a dog,
And when he told us about it, we were all agog.
So we thought about it,
Cos we weren't too sure
Then we decided it would help him mature
We talked it through and what it would be,
And how it would give him more responsibility
Then we brought him home, a tiny Labrador
Who skidded and poo'd and wee'd on the floor!
We had a chat with him our black ball of fluff
We put puppy pads down, and, sure enough,
He learned straight away to wee on one spot
We thought "he's a clever dog" (but not a lot!)
Connor wanted the name Doom or Grim
But we didn't fancy calling "Oi Grim come on in"
So he got the name Trevor (from GTA)
And it suits him cos he is (mostly) clever
And I must say, day by day, bit by bit,
He learned to beg and spin and sit
And we hid bits of food to play hide and seek
But oh what a wimp he is, so mild and meek.
We saw a "thing" in the garden a few weeks ago
We thought "ha! Trevor will sort it out" and so,
We said "Trevor go get it!"
It was a rat not a mouse,
He went outside, barked, then ran back in the house!

His favourite things are food and a ball
And his ears prick up and he stands up tall
When he hears the bowl put down on the floor,
We know that he loves us but he loves food more.
He skids and slides to his bowl in a dash
He slobbers and slurps then it's gone in a flash
Then he pushes his bowl around on the floor,
And looks pleadingly as if to say "Can I have more?"
We love our Trevor, our bundle of joy
We love his nature, such a gentle boy
When we come home and open the door,
We can hear his feet pounding the floor
And then he greets us with this waggly tail
Our worries and cares fall away without fail
And thinking about it when all's said and done,
He's one of the family and with him life's such fun.

**From 'Pieces of my Heart' anthology
by Elaine Gardner**

John Brookes

John is a well known character in Wallsend. He's a
member of various art groups in the North East.
He is always happy to encourage and support fellow
members.
John is also a keen Street Photographer and has an
impressive portfolio.

Is this artwork or a photograph?

Answer on page 99

My cat Ben

Ben is Burmese he never tries to please.
If he wants my attention
He will tap me on my shoulder
With the greatest of ease

When you take your shoes off beware
He likes to chase your feet, and you may fall in the air

I love it when he is asleep
Because you can hear his gentle snore
Maybe dreaming of fish and chicken
And so much more

When visitors come to call
He will meow to say hello
Then look at me, he is my protector
My heart is a glow.

That is why I love this unique, handsome cat so.

Linda Simcox

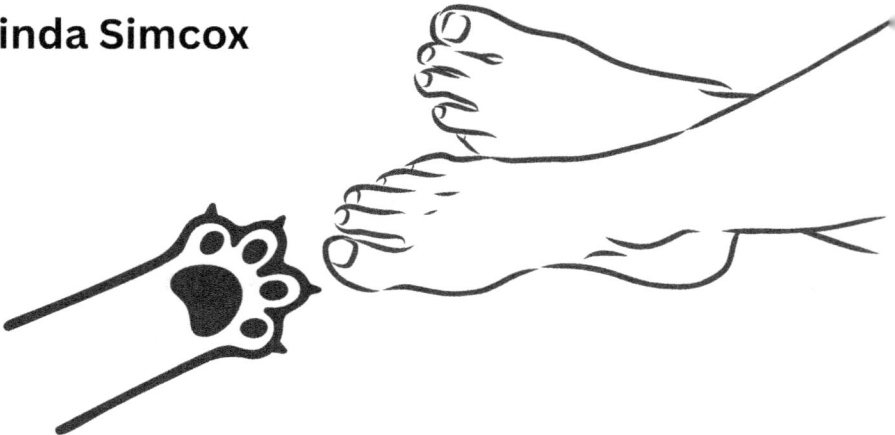

"Ben is very special because my son Paul said get a Burmese they are none vocal mam (he never shuts up telling me such stories in his cat language). My husband George bought him for my birthday he was 12 weeks old. Sadly my son and husband are no longer here Ben is now nineteen years old and is a big part of my life ."

Linda Simcox

Elvis

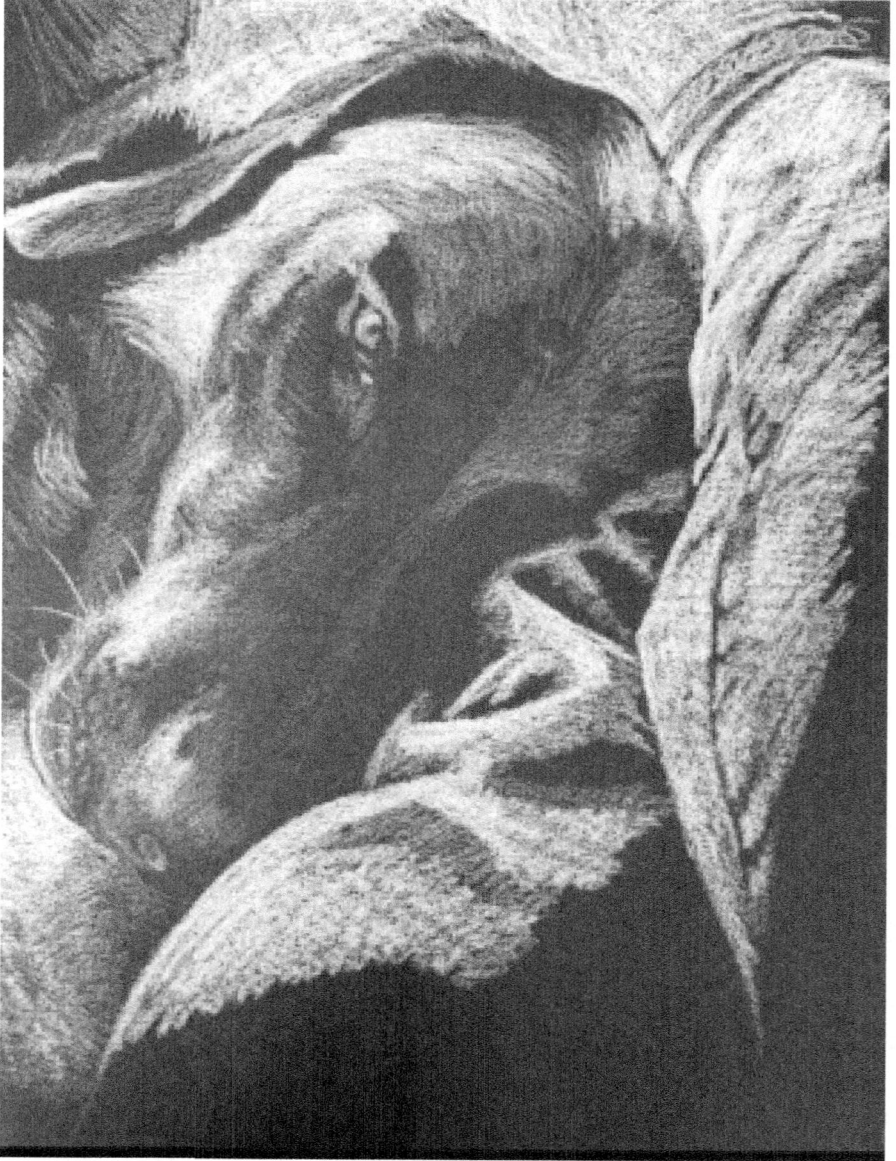

By Jane Kemp

Elvis

By Jane Kemp

Norma Patterson

"Nature is slow, but sure; she works no faster than need be; she is the tortoise that wins the race by her perseverance."

Henry David Thoreau

You Saved Me
(Dedicated to my beloved dog Dre)

You didn't have the best start
Battered, starved and neglected
Everyone was unsure
How you would be affected

As you trembled in the cage
Feeling frightened and alone
The minute I saw you
I knew I'd take you home

I held you as you quivered
And promised you'd be okay
You looked back with knowing eyes
We saved each other that day!

Wendy Jackson

25

Butterfly

Snatched on a
Wicked wind
And bullied
Tumbling
From beauty
Into noise and fog

Her vivid colour
Smudged
And greyed
With fumes
A pertinent vanity
Cowed with
Tearstained wings

Still
The breathless
Shadows plunge
To crush
Or cradle and
Keep
World through a window
A museum piece
Imprisoned
Till the hand that
Caught her
Spilled her
To the breeze
afresh

By Julie Meredith

Peggy Mace

Pup dog Mace
has a furry face
she leaves her toys
all over the place

Peggy Mace is a wonderful dog
If lots of sticks are around, she'll pick a log
Her eyes are always shining
With lots of love for her to bring
A beautiful tri-colour Border Collie
Who gives me everything

My Peggy is a delight to be had,
She'll have you laughing aloud, even when you're sad,
Her tail wagging, her beautiful smile,
She'll have you walk many a mile,
Always around to make you happy
Because for Peggy, that's her style.

Peggy Mace likes to steal your chair,
She is so cheeky you can't despair
Placing her toy just out of reach
You go get it, you've lost your seat
But now you're up it's time to play,
Always smiling, never missing a beat

Peggy Mace is just full of Joy
She knows the name of every toy
Ask for Colin, Dragon, Dino, Spider or bone
Off she'll trot, around our home
Looking merrily for the toy you asked for
She'll come in proudly with it to be thrown.

Peggy Mace is a wonderful dog
If lots of sticks are around, she'll pick a log
Her eyes are always shining
With lots of love for her to bring
A beautiful tri-colour Border Collie
Who will have us often sing:

Pup dog Mace has a furry face
she leaves her toys all over the place

By Becks Macey

Philip Barclay

"Aim to be like a rhino to have a single purpose, to charge at obstacles and goals with total commitment and to develop a thick skin to deal with the slings and arrows that try to slow you down"

Bear Grylls

Encounter

There, out of the corner of my eye
Only a second to turn
Speed at its swiftest
And then gone

From the slight hill
I stood and looked into the dip
But there was nothing
Just heather, and scrub bushes

Not a sign of movement
The brown flight no more
And looking, I would not find
Invisible to eyes only yards away

My one and only encounter
With a bird of wonder
But a treasured memory
Of my encounter with a merlin

George Richardson

Soulmate

She barks in anticipation
As I open the front door
Her excitement evident,
As her body quivers more
I am greeted with a gift
Which she places at my feet
I take it off her happily
And now she wants a treat
She follows me expectantly
As I make my cup of tea
My cuppa made, I settle down
And she snuggles into me
Her coat so soft and silky
With a champagne golden hue
And eyes so warm and friendly
As she gazes up at you
My life would not be the same
If she did not play her part
Does she know the impact
She leaves on my grateful heart

Mo Mitchell

A portrait of Maisie by P Mitchell

Paul is a local artist from Whitley Bay.
For more details of his work please see
Instagram: @pmitchellartworks
Email: pmitchellartworks@gmail.com

Artwork by Laura Young
You can find more artwork by Laura
on her Facebook page

Hungry Like
The Wolf

The wolf awakens from his deep sleep
Through the woods at night he will creep
The need for blood is top of his list
To find his prey he must persist
Animals scarper as he saunters along
This is his territory where he belongs
Licking his lips in anticipation
One false move could lead to frustration
He spots movement in a nearby bush
The hunt is on, he feels the rush
He launches forward his body tense
Then knocks himself out when he hits the fence

Dawn Wilkinson

The Platypus — A Reet Canny Beast

Here, sit yersel' doon, bonny lad —
and we'll have a wee bit craic.
Ah'll tell ye 'boot a beasty, mind,
that meks even clever lads step back.

Ye see, ah once seen this picture —
in a book me cousin had —
wi' a duck's heed and a beaver's arse,
ah thought, "Eeee! That's bloody radge!"

A platypus, they called it,
lives doon in Oz or there aboots,
half this, half that, half t'other —
and nee bugger knaas its roots!

It waddles like it's had a pint,
an' dives like it's Tom Daley,
lays eggs like hens on Sunday morn —
but feeds bairns milk from its own dairy!

"Ye're windin' us up," ah says,
"Ye cannit have that mix!"
but they swore it were real, like —
it's Nature's daftest fix.

It's got a poison spur, ye knaa,
on its leg, just there behind.
So if ye grab it when ye shouldn't,
ye'll soon be changed o' mind!

But it disn't bark or bleat,
nor crow, nor roar, nor hiss —
it just swims aboot all quiet-like,
in its private sort o' bliss.
An' ah thought, sittin' there starin',
wi' me pint an' me Dickson's pie,
mebbe that's the way to live, hinny —
just get on, be happy, divn't cry.
Nee argy-bargy, nee carry-on,
divn't gan thinkin' ye're a star —
just do what ye div best, pet,
be happy as ye are.
Aye —
the platypus is as strange as owt,
he's really as soft as clarts,
he waddles aboot wi' a big daft grin,
an' steals aal the lasses' hearts.
So 'cheers' to the weirdy platypus,
the daftest beast on Earth —
may we aal be a bit like him,
an' strive for all we're worth.

Aidan K. Morrissey

37

The Kitten And His Paws

One, two, three, four
The kitten counted his paws

'Yes that's right' my sweet mama said to me
'You have four paws just like me'

'But wait' I said *'What is this behind me?'*
'It's your tail my sweet boy' my mama told me

So I have four paws and I am so pleased
Because I thought I could only count to three

Sue Gray

Shandy

Our lovely dog Shandy shared our hearts and home
So I am telling you about her in this lovely poem

When my husband said 'I love you',
I thought it was for me
But when I looked around, he was talking to Shandy
Sitting on his knee

Having a dog like Shandy, she was not just a pet
The love and warmth she gave us we'll never forget

Her memory lingers on the days we had together
Taking her for walks, no matter what the weather

When Shandy crossed the rainbow bridge
we said to her goodbye
For days and days all we did was cry, and cry, and cry

We just could not replace her with another one
She broke our hearts you see the day that she was gone

So look after your pets they'll bring so much pleasure
As they will give you the memories to always treasure

Margaret Rose

Words Are Not Needed

If you could talk
What would you say?
There is no need
I know in your eyes
Or a tilt of your head
You need my attention
Whenever you put your chin on my lap
'I need you to play with my ball or my bubbles'
Stand by your bowl
That's all you need to do
No need to talk
I know my duty
Go to the back door in need of a wee
Or a black bag on my hand maybe!
No need for a clock on the wall
You know the time
I don't know how
Our routine is simple
Work, rest, and play
That's how we get by
Day by day.

Jackie Waddington

Fancy That

A holiday is what I need
But I've got a cat
Who can look after him?
"I will" said Jack *"with my wife Cath"*
Wearing her hat. **Fancy that!**

"We will come every day
Feed him, stroke him, and give him a pat"
Said Jack and Cath. Still wearing her hat.
Fancy that!

After a week I hurry back to my cat
Thinking he will come excitedly seeking
Behind the chair, he is shyly peeking
He slowly comes out

Quietly meowing. Oh dear! He's turned his back
And I don't think he is speaking
Now fancy that! He's thinking he's now
Jack and Cath's cat, still wearing her hat.
Fancy that!

After a day since I've been back
I feed him and stroke him and give him a pat
My cat is now purring asleep on my lap
It's all back to normal
Except for one thing
I now have to wear Cath's hat. **Fancy that!**

Mary Naylor

Little Jenny Wren

A bird on a wing
A Thrush who can sing
A Robin with a breast so red
A Seagull with it's cry
Soaring high up in the sky
And a pigeon that has just been bred

They're all birds of a feather
And no matter the weather
So beautiful, wild and free
Eating worms from the ground
There are those also found
Making nests high up in the trees

The Swallow that others will follow
The Blackbird, Magpie, and Crow
Flying high in the sky above us
Swooping down to the earth below

Two Turtle Doves, the meaning of love
The dawn chorus that wakes us all
The Yellow Bellied Finch and Blue Tit
And the Cuckoo with it's mating call

So many species of birds all around us
The Chicken and even the Hen
Buy my favourite of all
Is the one that I call
"My Little Jenny Wren"

Joyce Conway

43

The Peacock

Have you ever seen a wild Peacock?
In it's true terrain
Not on a manicured lawn
Looking all haughty and vain

But strutting down
A sun-dried lane
Wearing his crown
And feathered cloak
And six foot train

He stops
Down comes his head
Slightly to one side
Then tips up his beak
To give a piercing shriek

Then out fans
His majestic tail
In all it's outrageous slendour
It's a sight you will never forget
And always will remember

Sheila Berry

"I came face to face with him when he hopped off a six foot tall wall and wandered down a village road in Veirkala, Southern India."

Photos by Steve Murray

"The stag does not seek the crown; it wears it effortlessly, a symbol of the strength within."

Anne Cato

Tess Roxborough

Squirrel

Lovely squirrel red or grey
Collect your nuts on this cold day
You need to hide them before the frost
And get them buried at all cost
Remember last year when you had forgotten
And you ended up with your nuts all rotten

John Oxton

I'd Rather Have A Dog

My dog thinks he's the master here
Orders me round with a wag and a sneer
Fetch my dinner, fluff my bed
And while you're up scratch my head

He takes the sofa, spreads out wide
Leaves me perching on the side
At night he snores, I get no space
But he still looks cute with his furry face

Now people say *"Donna, find a man*
A bloke to love you, hold your hand"
But why on earth would I swap my pup
For some fella who leaves the loo seat up?

My dog won't cheat he won't complain
He doesn't vanish down the pub again
He's loyal, funny, and always near
And best of all he loves my ear

No football chants, no stinking socks
No sneaky glance at Tinder locks
Just wagging tails and happy paws
And kisses slobbered on my jaws

So here's my choice and here's my plan
I'll take a dog instead of a man
At least my pooch when all is said
Still lets me share a bit of the bed

Donna Peat

Cat Memories

The way that you woke me at six every morn
You climbed up the tree, and couldn't get down
You didn't approve when I spoke on the phone
And with loud meow, you let it be known
You walked on the keyboard or sat on my book
You wanted attention by hook or by crook

It was hard to leave you for more than a day
You struggled to cope when I went away
You hid in the suitcase that I'd just packed
You knew I was going and that is a fact
When I returned, you complained all day long
Made sure that I knew I had done something wrong

When I was alone you were good company
When I complained you listened to me
You may not have answered but that was fine
The warmth of your body curled up against mine
Allowed me to know that someone was there
To help me to cope with any despair

I wish one more time that I could see
You curled up close, next to me
Contented purrs I crave to hear
To remind me that you're still near
I'd listen to that friendly meow
If you were here
I miss you now

Linda Merritt

Sign

"Beware of the Dog" is what the sign says
Intrude here and it will be the end of your days
The postie knows better than to drop off bills
He's heard rumour of your tally of kills

Tradesmen fear coming to give your owner quotes
No matter how much Mummy bribes them with
used notes
Family haven't visited for many years
Your handiwork has had then all in tears

If only they knew the truth behind the sign
Despite the noise you are quite benign
Although your ancestors were tough as nails
Life on a cushion has turned you quite frail

Your barks and growls are high and shrill
Silence is the only thing you can kill
Your slightest growl should make my enemies fall
But the truth is, you're a Jack Russell,
and eight inches tall

Martin Wardle

Pippa

Rebecca Wardle

CHINA

Eyes that burned so bright are now dimmed,
Like the sun when by the Moon's shadow rimmed.
A life with so much love to give,
Now gone; but we still live.
No more the cuddles, no purring lap
No welcome meow, no tabby cat.
A part of us went with you,
Of how to cope, I have no clue.
Our hearts are now missing a piece,
No more purrs, but you are at peace.
You will live on, in our mind,
With the love that hearts do bind.

Steve Gore

10th October 2018. Written nine months after our
lovely old boy China, a rescue cat, at the age of 21,
went into The Remembering. I have had many, many
cats and mourn them all, but especially China. RIP
young man.

Roxy

Roxy the stray, all scruffy and small,
No one to love her, no home at all.
She had four kittens, each one a boy,
They found new families, they found joy.
But little Miss Roxy was left on the shelf,
No one came forward to love Roxy herself.
Till one special day, we sealed our fate,
we adopted each other on that December date.
She waltzed in my heart with a swish of her tail,
A purr like a song, and a spirit so hale.
Now Roxy's my shadow, my cuddle, my friend,
A bond that was written with no start or end.
So here we remain, my Roxy and me,
Together forever, it's meant to be.

Maureen Waters

57

Charlie and Milo

Charlie

My name is Charlie. My mum and dad call me chicken leg Charlie, (I possibly don't know what they could mean). I have yellow eyes and I love eating chillies and I like throwing them in the air and catching them. I cannot meow even when I was a little kitten, but I can still make my mam understand me. I was born in the Byker Wall when I was taken from my real mum at 6 weeks old. Then came along my adopted mum and dad and bought me for £50 and I have never looked back. They spoil me terrible and I had a life of riley sleeping all day and just being lazy, food on tap, it was like being in the Ritz. I dream a lot these days as I am 9 years old. Then one day this little kitten, a grey ball of fluff came into the house and my mam and dad said Charlie welcome to your new little brother Milo. Life has just not been the same since he arrived, he is always jumping on my back and pulling tufts of fur off me. You see I am a long hair tabby so my fur comes out easily. Every now and then I have to give him a bat to put him in his place to let him know that I am the alpha male. I have also got a twist in my tail. My mum used to say I was getting fat, but since Milo came I have been sprinting up and down the stairs, the exercise is killing me.

Charlie and Milo

Milo

My name is Milo, my mum calls me her little monkey. I am a British blue/mainecoon with green eyes and a silky grey coat. I am 2 years old and I love to run around the house and up and down my tower. When the runner in the hallway has been hoovered I run at it thinking it is a rabbit and I ruffle it up. I love doing that, but I get told off. I don't care, I still do it. I love playing in the sink with the water from the tap splashing everything. I have a big brother called Charlie. I love getting him wet with the water. He is so boring I mean really boring. He won't even play with me. He always wants to go to sleep or stuff his fat face. He only wants to play when it suits him well, I am not having it. He pins me down and bites my neck and then licks me to death with his smelly fishy breath. I do love him loads but I wish I was in charge and the big boss not him. My mum said to Charlie and me one day if it rains or paws I am all yours. You have got all my love. I didn't know what she meant then, but I definitely do now.

Karen Marchetto

> *"The horse, the horse! The symbol of surging potency and power of movement, of action."*

D. H. Lawrence

Ben Tasker

Ged Hazlehurst

"*What greater gift than the love of a cat*"

Charles Dickens

Be More Dog

I wish I could be more like my dog
And not have a care in the world
Eat, sleep, play games and repeat
To lie in a ball or uncurled

My dog doesn't worry about finances
He doesn't have to go out to work
He isn't caught up in the capitalist game
Bills are a thing he can shirk

Neither is he concerned with the newest of things
He's happy with a ball he can catch
And no matter how much he is caught in the moment
Everything stops for a scratch

He isn't so taken with new clothes
A collar is his only suit
And it doesn't matter what car he's in
They all look the same from the boot.

His food doesn't have to be gourmet
He just wants it there in his dish
He isn't too fussed if it's jellied or dry
Something to eat is his wish

And oh, how exciting are walks?!
I should start to follow his lead
I want to experience what he does
When his leash is unclipped and he's freed

Liam Overend
@JustLiamPoetry

Photos kindly submitted by Christiane Laura Jane Shillito, from her 2025 Safari adventure and trip to Turtle Sanctuary, Zanzibar Island

There Was A Young Boy

There was a young boy called Yogi
He used to keep all his bogies
This big pile of goo
Stuck together like glue
And frightened his cat called Toby

Steve Wraith

The Guardian

Gina entered the front door wearing the skirt, shirt, jacket and heels she had worn at work before shouting up the stairs "Glenn, sorry I'm late love. Can't be bothered with making dinner tonight, so I'll pop around to Talbot Street Chip shop for us."

Further up the street from where Gina and Glenn live, three young men in hoods were acting like predatory animals as they menacingly prowled around the built-up housing estate in the dark on their bikes. They acted like they controlled the place, but since their appearance stopped anyone passing by or going near – they essentially do.

With her smart jacket swapped for her all-weather coat "I'll just get my purse" and the scrape of a bunch of keys off the shelf she headed back out the front door.

They were hanging around the bottom end of one of many narrow pedestrian alleys between homes that connected streets on the estate and looking for money – other people's money. One of them alerted the others as a young lady appeared at the top entrance of the alley in the dim street-light and clutching what could be a handbag or purse in her hand.

Seeing the cycles charging towards her Gina froze at the end of alley going no further, but more than that, she can sense something is wrong - but it's too late to do anything about it.

The hooded boys silently hurtled towards her through the narrow alley on their bikes. The lead hoodie already had his eye on grabbing her handbag and committed to crashing into her to allow the others to take her bag. To his horror and confusion, he tried to stop, but it was too late - he realised it wasn't a handbag but a retractable dog lead.

His panic was compounded when he saw that at the other end of the lead was a large male Belgian Sheppard that sprinted around the corner as soon as he heard a threat to his mistress.

A deathly squeeze of brakes from behind the lead hoodie, sounded just before the clattering of the three bikes piling on top of each other in the narrow confines at the end of the alley. After some frantic shouting and profanity, the surprised cyclists untangled themselves from each other and their bikes as Gina stepped backwards and out of the alley, leaving the dog to remind the would-be attackers that his mistress's safety was his responsibility.

With the loudest and most terrifying display of teeth and athletics and the tearing of jackets and hoods the disgruntled dog made his displeasure known to the three cyclists as they took off in all directions minus their bikes.

That evening Glenn got his favourite treat with his supper: two battered smokey sausages from the fish and chip shop roughly chopped and topped his usual meat and biscuit – just the way he likes it. And as Gabby was putting down the bowl and Glenn tore into his treat – she couldn't help but marvel on how intuitive dogs were.

Simon Waim

Maple

Maple is so sweet
She's made my life complete
She's white with a tabby tail
She makes me smile without fail
She loves when you stroke her tummy
She thinks pork is so yummy
She will give you kisses to brighten your day
But wake you in the night to check you're okay
She's my best furry friend
The love I have, others can't comprehend

Maple is my sun, moon, and stars

Poem and picture below by
Grace Hedley (Aged 9)

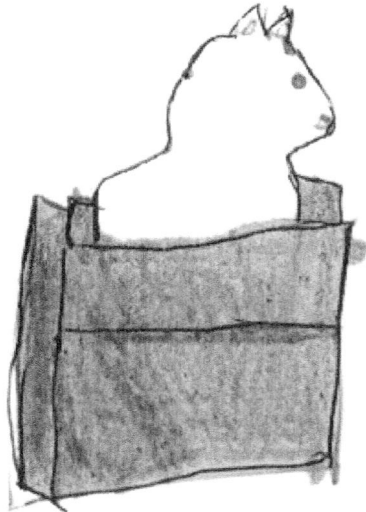

Dido

Dido is my rabbit and I love him
with all my heart
Since the very start
When I'm sad Dido makes me feel better
And if I'm lucky he will lick me on the nose
Dido is very fluffy in the winter
But when Summer comes he sheds all over me
But when that happens I can give him a big brush
I'll always love him
And I bet he loves me too

Poem and picture below by
Pip Underwood (Aged 9)

Bruno

Bruno came to me when I was three
I love to have him on my knee
His fur is dark grey and white
Eyes green and oh so bright
He sleeps all day
On the radiator, he loves to lay
Brings us mice as a treat
Tune and chicken he likes to eat
He is my very best friend
And I will love him to the end
Bruno, Bruno, I love you
And I know you love me too

**Poem and picture above by
Alice Hedley (Aged 9)**

Bob

Ginger fur and cute white paws,
He came along when I needed him most.

A cute little stray with coal black eyes,
long lashes and a cute kitty smile.

My little friend, his paw holds my hand,
I tell him all I have planned.

No response from him, none required,
let's snuggle down and mind each other.

Cats don't care people say,
they stalk around awaiting treats
haughty looks and loud meows.

My Bob is different I always say my furry friend
until the end.

Leeanne Rooney

A Moment's Trance

I grabbed the lead, this showed intent,
he knew exactly what it meant.
A swishing tail, a gleeful jig,
Yeah Jasp was ready for the gig.
So off we set upon our jaunt,
Through Battle Hill's familiar haunts.
Past my old school of early years,
onto the cinder path that's there.
We followed eastwards for a spell,
then took a track I know so well.
Where butterflies in flight would dance,
and hold me in a moment's trance.
The bramble bushes groaned with fruit,
at every juncture on this route.
We bowled along and stride for stride,
my faithful friend was by my side.
Around and round no mind to stop,
until we'd reached the very top.
And once we did I looked around,
and what a splendid view I'd found.
The monument on Penshaw hill,
and Pontop Pike yet higher still.
And to the North highest of all,
The Cheviots so seemed to call.
Past West Allotment's quiet charm,
we headed west to Scaffold Farm.
So many memories flooded back,
along this so familiar track.

Back on the homeward journey now,
as sun shone on my freckled brow.
Upon the pit surveying the scene,
a sea surrounds us, purest green.
Waves seem to lash upon our bow,
but safe our haven is and how.
Descending down a well-worn track,
our weary legs are heading back.
Past my old haunts the good old dene,
where once there was a bowling green.
The lead back on now last few strides,
our tiredness is hard to hide.
Then home at last, a welcome sight.
By God we both shall sleep tonight.

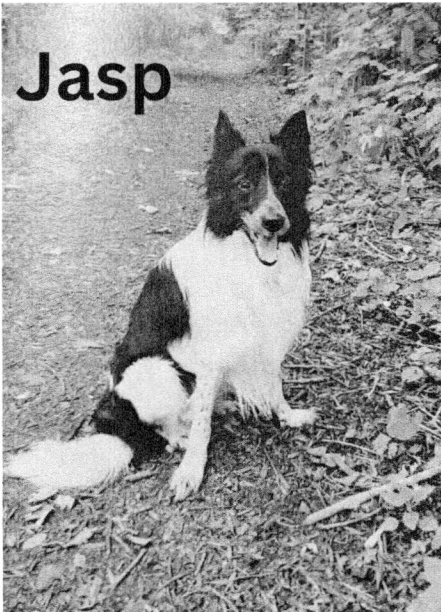

Jasp

**James Bridgewood
(from 'The Rhyme of
My Life' available now
on Amazon)
'Bright Red' Also
Available**

A GEORDIE'S LIFE
IN RHYME

AN ANTHOLOGY OF POEMS
BY
JAMES BRIDGEWOOD

bright
red

Fighting blood cancer
for a brighter future

Milo

Purring like a car engine.
Batting me for attention.
Eating several helpings of food a day . . .
Forever hungry.
Placing his soft paw on me,
to keep physical contact.
Kneeding me like dough.
Climbing on my side when I sleep.
My constant companion.
A reason to get out of bed.

My lovely Milo

Jo Crawford

Pandemonium

"Hello there, who's a pretty boy then?" are the words I often hear
As a high-pitched tone and repetitive words glide into my hidden ear.
A heavily lined, aged smiling face greets me every day.
Hanging on to my every chirp eagerly waiting to hear what I might say!

I like to have fun with him and put on an act.
After all I'm a master of mimicry, I'm super intelligent, that's a fact.
I use my muscular tongue and throat muscles to help pronounce words and phrases
As I delight with all his impressed oohs and ahhs and captivated gazes.

He always makes a huge fuss of me when his home help comes.
He delights in telling her what tricks I've performed as he puts his false teeth in between his gums.
At lunch time he nibbles on his sandwich, two pieces of bread and a slice of ham.
Then he comes over to my cage
with a handful of nuts and feeds me them
asking me how I am?

I like it when he puts on his vintage radio and says "Come on boy let's see you move"
Songs from the 1950's play and I get into my unique parrot groove.
Head bobbing and shaking my colourful plumage, I create my own dance.
His tired face lights up and he suddenly beams, giving me a very proud glance

In the early evening I enjoy my flying time and before I return to my cage,
I often sit on his shoulder when he is reading and I help turn the page.
At bedtime he covers my cage with an old flowery cotton sheet then he wishes me a loving 'Goodnight my bonny lad'.
I repeat to him and chirp 'Goodnight my bonny lad' he's the best friend I have ever had.

We have been companions for over thirty years
When the house was full of voices.
Now it's just him and I making our very own pandemonium and noises.

A man and his lifelong friend a parrot like nothing better than a good natter.
You see we have our very own special bond where the language barrier really doesn't matter.
He tells me his worries, his secrets and all his hopes and dreams.
A best friend can have feathers and wings, I'm not just his pet like it seems.

Clare McAndrew

Artwork by Christopher Younger
You can find more artwork by Christopher
on his Facebook page

Maisie

She came as a rescue
a mystery as to how
she has only 3 legs
as she timidly

arrived
with her 3 white socks
and her pistachio green eyes
watching me

from across the room
from under the bed
distrust in her eyes
my heart had to wait

for the precious moment

when scrambling onto my bed
she stared
as if she had known
me forever

now she sleeps by my side
or curled up on my back
delicately snoring
mysterious cat

Lesley Armour

Maisie

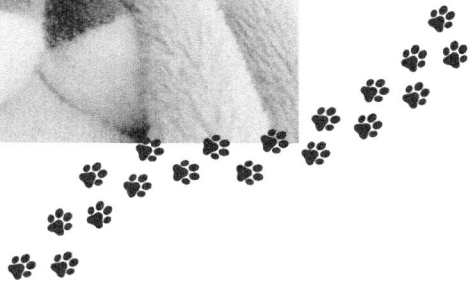

"*Owners of dogs will have noticed that, if you provide them with food and water and shelter and affection, they will think you are god. Whereas owners of cats are compelled to realize that, if you provide them with food and water and shelter and affection, they draw the conclusion that they are gods.*"

Christopher Hitchens

Eric

Forever a morning creature,
You rush to the opening door,
Desperate for affection,
Purring your greeting of love.
Chattering, tail curling around my leg,
Like a ribbon full of static.
As I stiffly bend to the ground,
Talking in a language you undoubtably understand.
Yawning, crispy-eyed,
Craving some of the morning persona you wear so well.
You stretch, then bounce off your front paws,
Head touching my hand as I sit on the carpet,
Close to you, mountain and tree.
Kissing your apricot-coloured head,
Inhaling the fragrance of your fur,
As you purr like the engine,
Of the world's finest car.
Paw to my face,
Telling me you love me,
As you headbutt my cheek.
And you do love me,
As I love you.
The cat-shaped hole in my heart,
Now filled.

Helen Aitchison

If you would like to see what Eric is up to, you can find him on TikTok, Facebook, Instagram, and X; **Eric's Escapades**

You can also find more information about Eric here:
www.writeonthetyne.com/eric

Eric's mammy, Helen Aitchison is an author who has books available on Amazon:

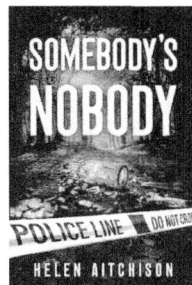

Ode To Cranes

Crane of commerce, rusty, tall.
Cranefly of the insect world, fluorescent, small.

You both appear in my field of view. One is old, one is
new.

One was industry,
the other industrious, learning to fly, from the water,
where lillies lie.

Andy Allum

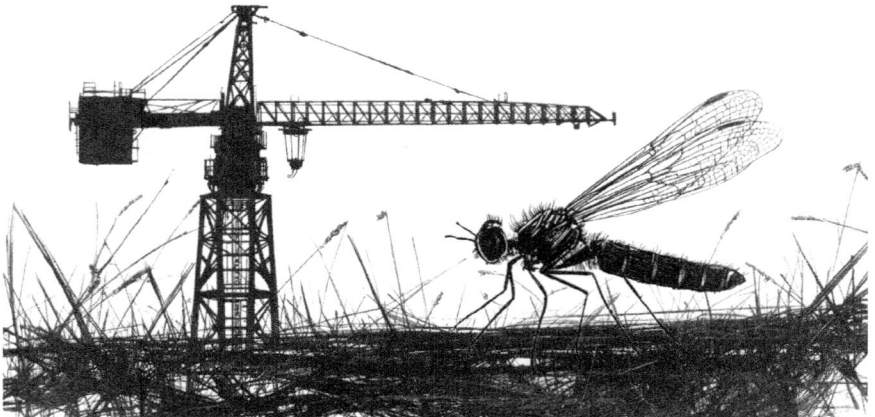

Cheekie

My metal cat Cheekie, a reminder of a dear sister, Stella
true
It stands to remind me of days spent with you
From Nelson town, which I saw as a happy find
Now a treasure, to treasure for my mind
With plant, shape of such feline grace
It smiles at me with whiskers and tail in its new place
Herbs can grow, flowers will bloom oh so bright
A reminder of Nelson with such pure delight
With a white rose charm in metal form
Pusa keeps my memories alive, safe and warm
With each glance at my cat my heart gratefully fills
Rusty but sturdy with whiskers that gleam
It watches over the flowers like in a dazzling dream
A home for plants and flowers tender and bold
In the arms of Cheekie stories can unfold
In metal and soil my memories grow
From Nelson town it embraces where fond memories
flow

Barry Martin

85

Riverbank

Come down to the river as last of daylight fades
There it's cool and peaceful and safe in verdant shade
Wildlife gathers at the stream where water fresh
cascades
The badgers shuffle and snuffle in the sanctity of the
glade

Peeping through the clearing is a deer with velvet eyes
Hiding quietly under the cover of camouflage disguise
Leaves fly on the breeze, a sudden noise causes
surprise
Her long strong legs spring towards a new place to hide

A russet fox comes for a look to see what he might find
Slinking around with nose to the ground then glancing
behind
To check the shrubs and bushes leading to where it's
tree-lined
Wondering what's on the supper menu, food occupies
his mind

Red squirrels leap and play, keeping busy all through
the day
Scurrying along, climbing trees they're so fast at getting
away
Essential foraging for fungi, nuts and berries, it's not all
play
Storing away treats for the winter cache cannot be
delayed.

Spotted woodpeckers drum and cuck and willow warbler tweets
The others augment the orchestra with eclectic songs and beats
Come back to nature, it's waiting to make you feel complete
Love our wildlife, flora and fauna in a place of peaceful retreat

Angela Craddock

ORNITHORHYNCUS ANATINUS

There's a big building in Newcastle
That's called the Lit and Phil.
It has been there for two hundred years,
Near the bottom of Westgate Hill.
It is owned by a Society
Concerned with thoughts and books.
It has a massive library there
For everyone who looks.
Twenty years before it opened
Or maybe a little more,
They were given a small animal
That no one else had seen before.
It came from a man called Hunter,
Governor of New South Wales.
It only weighed three or four pounds
When they put it on the scales.
They looked at it very closely,
Because they thought it was a fake.
The back looked like a Beaver,
But the front looked like a Drake!
No one could quite believe it,
It was certainly far-fetched.
The like of it had ne'er been seen.
Their credulity was stretched.
Apart from its appearance,
It had two more striking features,
That it didn't share with any of
The world's more unusual creatures.

It had nipples where the baby one
Could feed on warm milk from the mother,
But the babes themselves hatched out from eggs
Like their sister and their brother.
It took quite a lot of getting used to,
But the experts all agreed
That they'd call it a "Duck-billed Platypus"
Which was clever of them indeed.
As time went on they studied them
Until they came to understand
That they were as much at home in the water
As they were at home on land.
Its beak could scoop up lots of food,
Like insects, tadpoles, shrimps and such,
Transferring them into its mouth
All done by sense of touch.
The front paws being equipped with webs
Had the experts quite confused
Because they were retractable
When they weren't being used.
"A horse designed by a committee"
Someone once defined a camel.
Then please describe the company who
Designed this bird/ fish/ mammal!

Kenn Creen

Best Friends

Phyllis Benoist

The following two pieces have been submitted by Clare Metcalf. Sadly, Clare recently lost her beloved cat, Jasper, while I was putting this book together. I reached out to Clare to ask if she would like to contribute a poem for this book, she responded with two deeply moving pieces that capture both the spirit and story of Jasper in a truly heartfelt way.

Her first poem beautifully encapsulates Jasper's personality — his quirks, his charm, and the quiet comfort he brought to those around him. It paints a vivid picture of a cat full of character, mischief, and warmth. The second piece, written from Jasper's own imagined perspective, is especially poignant. Through Jasper's "voice," Clare shares a tender farewell that speaks of love, loyalty, and the unbreakable bond between pet and owner. Reading it brought tears to my eyes, as it so perfectly expresses the bittersweet mixture of gratitude and grief that comes with saying goodbye.

Animals bring immeasurable love, joy, and companionship into our lives. They ask for so little in return, yet give us everything — comfort, laughter, and unconditional affection. As Paul O'Grady's quote at the beginning of this book reminds us, the heartache we endure when we lose them is the price we pay for that love. Clare's words are a touching tribute not only to Jasper but to all the animals who leave pawprints on our hearts long after they are gone.

Dawn Wilkinson

Jasper

My love is ginger, orange, cream and amber
Striped like a tiger, with soft silken fur
10 pink toe-beans, so soft and tender
He's my special angelic broken heart-mender

His eyes aglow like rich amber jewels
Deep and golden, unblinking pools
Magnificent whiskers, so long and unique
White and black, caressing my cheek

A gentle purr, no husky deep rumble
Sweet, thoughtful, shy and humble
His voice whose pitch can rise rather high
At times, sounds softer than a sigh

Kiss my cheek, he'd always demand
Then kiss the other -- it's what I had planned
Kiss my forehead, just like my Cat Mummy
Then kiss me again, you know I'm so funny

I've two more cheeks for you to kiss
Here they are, be sure you don't miss
It makes us both laugh, he's such a funny guy
And I love it too, don't ask me why

Born with extra bendy joints
He's super flexible at certain points
Around my neck he furls his tail
His own special hug, my heart melts without fail

Not all understand our special bond
But all those who meet him become so fond
Of my Orange boy with soft amber eyes
And gentle voice, and purring sighs

Clare Metcalf

My Name Is Jasper

My name is Jasper, and I'm an angel. Not just because I'm in Heaven now; I've always been an angel.

My big sister Lucy, who arrived here in Heaven years ago, chose me for my Mummy. She said my Mummy needed me as much as I was going to need her.

The day I was born there was much fuss and celebration. You see, my feline Mum, Daisy had been found at a building site and taken to somewhere called a Rescue, but I only ever knew it as Aunty Sue's house, where we all felt safe.

Life was sweet for me, my Mum and siblings, safe at Aunty Sue's house. My new Mummy visited every few days so we could get to know each other properly, and we were definitely falling in love.

Until when I was 4 weeks old, someone called a V.E.T. decided I wasn't perfect, that my hips were deformed (dysplasia) and that I'd never be able to walk, run, or go to the toilet unassisted. He wanted to kill me there and then. But he didn't realise my Mummy is a lioness for her babies, and she insisted I come straight home, where she gave me magic pills – homey something or other – (Homeopathy) and before long I was proving that man wrong at every turn. There was almost a party the day I pooped by myself!

A few weeks later I came home with Mummy, Daddy and my grumpy big sister Dusty, and life was great, but I proved a bit too lively for Dusty, so I was allowed to pick a baby brother to play with, and home came Barney. We had the MOST fun, and quite a few cuddles too, but don't tell anyone we're softies!

And I helped my Mummy heal when her own Daddy got sick and then went to Heaven. She says I healed her heart, her orange angel. One good turn deserves another, I say. And I was the goodest of good boys, never put a paw wrong and spread love to everyone who met me. Not fond of being picked up or hugged, I gave the best kisses, and I was most generous with them, if I liked a person. I'd hug Mummy with my prehensile tail.

I loved to run and climb and leap like a gazelle and sit in the highest spot. I loved sunrises and sunsets and listening to the birds singing. And I loved rainbows. They seemed to find me wherever I napped. I even had a catnip rainbow I adored.

Then one day I just felt very sick out of nowhere, and before any of us realised what was happening, I was called back to Heaven again. I was 14 ½ years old. Mummy says it wasn't long enough, but it was 14 ½ years I may never have had. And now I look after everyone from Heaven, until we're all together again. In the meantime, look for me in rainbows and pretty skies, and birdsong, and cry for yourself if you need to, but also smile because we had so long together, and it was all pawfect.

Jasper Metcalf
(AKA Mr Whiskerly)
28th March 2011 – 19th October 2025
Only ever on loan from the Angels.

Clare's book 'Conversations with Bentley, the Cosmic, Conservationist Cat' is available on Amazon and also direct from her website;
www.freespiritanimalcare.co.uk

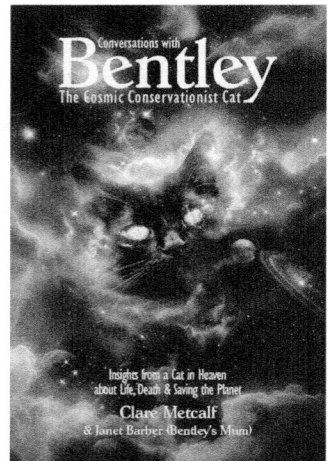

Conversations with
Bentley
The Cosmic Conservationist Cat

Insights from a Cat in Heaven
about Life, Death & Saving the Planet
Clare Metcalf
& Janet Barber (Bentley's Mum)

Thankyou   A heartfelt thank you to everyone who submitted their incredible work for the first volume of *'For the Love of Animals'*. The response has been truly overwhelming, with an outpouring of beautiful poems, touching short stories, and inspiring artwork that capture the spirit, loyalty, and joy animals bring into our lives. Each submission reflected a deep love and respect for the animal world, making this collection a true celebration of that bond.

The creativity and compassion shared through these pages have been so inspiring that work on Volume Two is already underway. The enthusiasm and talent of contributors have shown just how many people share a passion for animals and their welfare. Every piece, whether written or illustrated, has helped shape a book that not only entertains but also makes a difference.

The purpose of *'For the Love of Animals'* is to honour the beauty, wisdom, and companionship that animals bring to humanity. Beyond celebrating their presence, this project aims to give back to them in a meaningful way. All profits from this book will go towards establishing local pet food banks and supporting animal charities, helping to ensure that pets and their families receive the care and resources they need.

Gratitude extends to everyone who has supported this project—contributors, readers, and those spreading the word.

Each act of kindness helps build a stronger community of animal lovers dedicated to compassion and care.

To stay connected and follow updates on pet food bank initiatives, upcoming events, and future volumes, join the Facebook group 'For the Love of Animals'. It's a space for sharing stories, celebrating animals, and continuing the mission of kindness that inspired this book.

For anyone inspired to contribute to future volumes, submissions are always welcome. Reach out through the Facebook group to share poems, stories, or artwork that reflect the love and wonder animals bring to life.

Together we can make a difference!

Dawn Wilkinson

"He who is cruel to animals becomes hard also in his dealings with men. We can judge the heart of a man by his treatment of animals."

Immanuel Kant

Artwork or Photograph?

This is a piece of artwork submitted by John Brookes

Printed in Dunstable, United Kingdom

71677595R00057